Pin it, Pat it

Written by Charlotte Raby and
Emily Guille-Marrett
Photographed by Will Amlot

Collins

Dip it. Dip it.

Tip it in.

tin

Tap it. Pat it.

Tap a tin.

tin

Pin pin pin it.

Tap tap tap it.

Pat pat pat it.

Sit in it. Sit!

It is dim. Sit.

Tip it in. Tip.

Dip it in.

Nip at it.

14

🐾 After reading 🐾

Letters and Sounds: Phase 2

Word count: 48

Focus phonemes: /s/ /a/ /t/ /p/ /i/ /n/ /m/ /d/

Common exception word: is

Curriculum links: Understanding the World: People and Communities

Early learning goals: Understanding: answer "how" and "why" questions about their experiences and in response to stories or events; Reading: children read and understand simple sentences, use phonic knowledge to decode regular words and read them aloud accurately, read some common irregular words

Developing fluency

- Your child may enjoy hearing you read the book.
- Encourage your child to read the book again, this time acting out the actions. You may wish to model reading the first few pages like this and ask your child to continue with the rest of the book.

Phonic practice

- Help your child to practise sounding out and blending CVC words containing the /d/ sound.

  d/i/m   dim

  d/i/p   dip

- Look at the "I spy sounds" pages (14–15). Say the sound together. How many items can your child spot with the /d/ sound in them? (e.g. *dog, digger, dinosaur, drum, dragonfly, doll, drink, drawings, dancing*)

Extending vocabulary

- Read your child each set of words below. Which one is the odd one out?

  tip   pour   tin   (*tin*)

  sit   bite   nibble   (*sit*)

  dim   light   dark   (*light*)